For the Souls of the Departed:

A brief history & sampling of Portuguese folk magic.

Darlene A. Sousa, Ph.D.

First Edition
2006
ISBN 978-1-4303-0265-0

For the Souls of the Departed:

A brief history & sampling of Portuguese folk magic.

Introduction

Although Portugal and its islands the Acores and Madeira are considered predominately Catholic, many of the beliefs and practices so intertwined in everyday life there are the result of many non-Catholic influences. In particular with the islands of the Acores and Madeira, as is the case with so many island civilizations such as Madagascar, the Canary Islands, Cuba, and Puerto Rico, a blending of natural folk magic, superstitions, traditions of the African Diaspora introduced with the practices of the slave trade, and the imposed religion of the region, syncretism becomes a basis for the way of life.

In mingling with various spiritual groups the past several years, I find I am often met with curiosity by individuals who are of Portuguese descent or who know of someone Portuguese. These individuals plead for more information on the unusual and rather enchanting practices I mention, or have recollections of family members burning garlic, hanging horseshoes over doorways, or other such curious practices. The responses I receive are always usually to the effect of "I always knew she was a witch" when individuals learn that these practices are no way affiliated with the National religion.

I have spent much of my free time researching the basis for the spiritual and cultural practices of the Portuguese, and my discoveries have been complex and fascinating. In this book, I will share a little of the history of the Portuguese who have developed influential communities in Hawaii, California, Oregon, and much of the East Coast of the United States, as well as international communities in Canada, Southern and Western Africa, India, China, and South America. Further, theories for the basis of Portuguese mystical practices, along with several examples, spells, and recipes will be offered.

It is my hope in writing this book that I can provide some basic answers to those who are curious as to the practices they've encountered, a place to begin in the continuation of their hereditary rituals, and a spark of curiosity to those who have never encountered a Portuguese community and the means from which to perhaps validate their calling to folk magic.

Chapter 1:

A Basis for the Beliefs

So much in history has affected the ethnic make-up and cultural practices of the people who we now call the Portuguese. In fact, many Portuguese are unaware that much of the language they speak has its basis in Greek and Arabic. The geographic location of continental Portugal along with the Acores and Madeira islands in the Atlantic provided accessibility to the people and practices of the Celts, Africa, Greece, and Persia.

Although Portugal became an independent country in 1065 C.E., a thorough history of Portugal should start with the rule of the Phoenicians in 1104 B.C.E. From then on, a continuation of external influences played a role in the development of the current culture. The Celts left proof of their existence in Portugal by establishing monoliths, of which the most impressive is the Anta Grande do Zambujeiro (The Grand Dolmen of Zambujeiro) located near the city of Evora. In fact, this monolith is the largest dolmen in all of Europe.

Other influential events include the Moorish rule of Iberia (which means "West" in Arabic) leaving a lasting impression on language, tradition, cuisine, and even architecture. By strict definition, Moors are those who practice Islam of North African descent.

The regrettable inception of the slave trade by the Portuguese introduced the belief systems of the West and South African people. Although the Portuguese imposed this horrible practice upon the people of Africa, many Portuguese, especially those in the Acores, openly welcomed Africans who were removed from their motherland. Interracial marriage was common and thus began the incorporation of the belief system of the Yoruban and in particular, the Congo and Angolan people. The Spanish Inquisition and World War II both forced Gypsies, Jews, and others fleeing persecution over the Pyrenees into Portugal, and especially the Acores and Madeira islands where the waters of the Atlantic provided a protective buffer from the treacherous events of history we have all become familiar with.

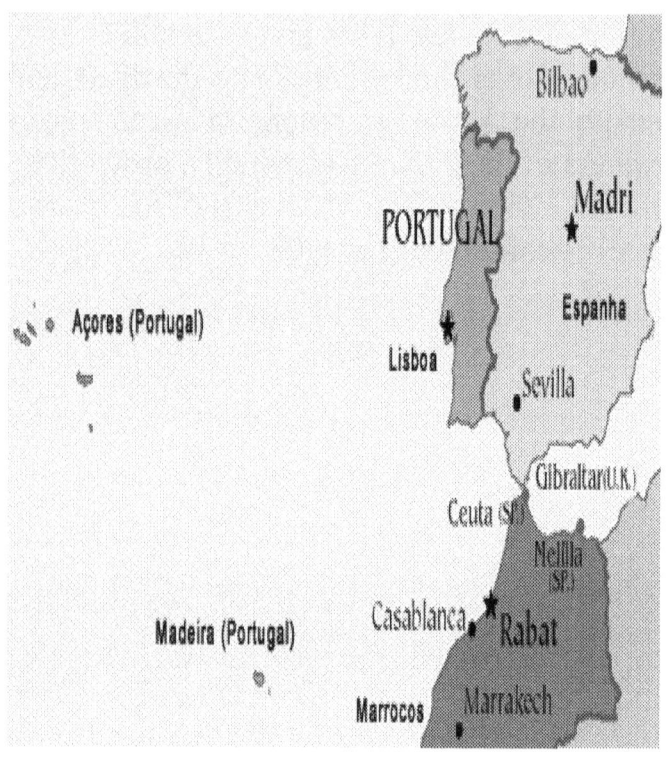

There is even speculation among some anthropologists that the Greeks introduced the first agrarian practices to the region. Theory has it that the Greeks used carved out logs as canoes and successfully fled their homeland, bringing with them the now familiar Portuguese products of figs, dates, nuts, and other agricultural staples. In fact, there are some who believe that the word Portugal comes from the Greeks who called their new port Kalles/Cale, meaning beautiful. Hence, Porto Kalles.

Thus, with only this brief introduction into the historical influences of Portugal and its islands, it becomes clear that the people and practices of this country have been influenced by so many different groups and events within history. This becomes evident in the physical appearances of the Portuguese who can range from fair and green eyed in the north, to olive toned with coarse raven hair in the southern regions.

It becomes only logical to then connect the collection of spiritual and magical practices found throughout the regions of Portugal to the external influences as well. With each new introduction of people and cultures came the influences of new blood and new forms of spirituality.

Hidden Beliefs

I have titled this section Hidden Beliefs since many of the beliefs to follow are commonly held by individuals in Portugal, particularly in the countryside and the islands, but are either not openly discussed or referenced in crypto-semantic euphemisms. In fact, many Portuguese are unaware that these beliefs and practices are anything but Catholic until they come to the United States and discuss them with a clergy member trained in true Catholicism, and are quite often times met with firm correction.

Many of the Portuguese communities on the West and East Coasts of the U.S. are founded by Acorean immigrants who established their own community centers to include chapels and churches. These churches are quite commonly staffed by clergy who were either educated in the "old country" or are descendents of the immigrants, and continue to promote these non-Catholic beliefs.

One of the first examples of this I ran into was regarding the belief in reincarnation. My mother had always made reference to reincarnation, particularly with regard to her mother who she was very close to. In casual conversation, around the age of 10, I mentioned reincarnation to an American priest who immediately attempted to correct my thinking on the topic of the afterlife. I was thoroughly confused; how could this man be correct when all of the conversations regarding the afterlife up to that point in my life consisted of the possibility of returning to this world in another body?

Furthermore, it is believed that the fate of the souls of the departed can be affected by the actions of the living. It is customary to offer a gift of food to a neighbor or a friend for the soul of the departed. Likewise, a gift or favor can be accepted with the recipient offering a thank you towards the soul of the gift giver's dearly departed. These offerings to the souls of the departed are believed to decrease the suffering of the departed during their transition to the next life, or on the way to the soul's final resting place. Be sure to try some of the recipes located at the end of the book which are commonly used as such offerings.

Dreams and their meanings are another significant hidden belief. It is believed that answers to dilemmas, insight into the future, and communication with the dead can all be achieved during sleep in the form of dreams. Many Portuguese will take their dreams so seriously as to become affected in their waking hours pondering the meaning to an unusual dream. It is not unusual to find a Portuguese rearranging plans due to the hidden message of a dream from the night before.

Dreams of flight are associated with what is commonly referred to as Astral Projection, whereas symbolism can be associated with outcomes; losing one's teeth in a dream foretells of the death of a family member. The night of the full moon is particularly fruitful to the anticipating dream reader. Although these dreams are personal and usually not shared with others, their prophetic significance and symbolic meanings manage to continue through the generations.

The Portuguese also believe that certain individuals are better endowed than others with the ability to foretell the future, "read" a person, and other matters mystical. These skills are usually first noticed as a child. Unlike the response in the U.S. whereas a family would think such ramblings from a child are all part of the youth's fantasy mind, or the effect of too much television, children in Portugal are revered, rewarded, and taken very seriously for their insight and intuitive abilities. It is believed their unfettered egos and untarnished souls provide them with a clearer connection to the mystical world.

Envy, curses, and the evil eye…need I say more? Like the gypsies, Moroccans to the south, and many others of the world, the fear of curses and the dreaded evil eye are a huge consumption of mental energy for the Portuguese. Envy is believed to be so powerful a force, as to be at fault for the failing of many attempted endeavors and relationships. Envy leads to the transfer of negative energy directed at the envied individual, which is believed to have the power to cause failed engagements, illness, poverty, accidents, and even death. It is quite common to withhold information of upcoming plans until the metaphorical eggs have hatched, so as to prevent any ill harm on the part of someone who may become envious of your plans.

Beyond envy is the curse. Whereas envy may be unintentional and possibly passive, a curse is the aggressive wishing that someone fail, become ill, or worse. It is believed that to look into the "evil eye" of someone cursing you is to guarantee the wish to come true. Hence, the concept of protective amulets, ritual cleansing, and the defensive hand gesture which will all be discussed in a later section of the book.

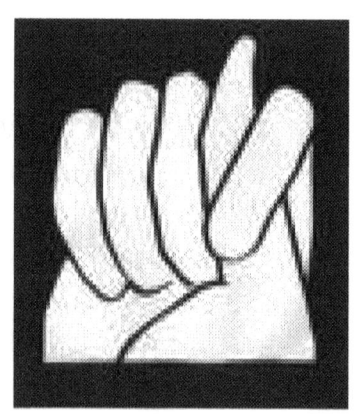

A brief history & sampling of Portuguese folk magic.

The following section contains several of the most commonly known practices among the Portuguese that have a basis in folk magic and mysticism. In the next few pages you will find instruction on divination, spells, holiday practices, rituals, several common herbal remedies, and delicious recipes for the Portuguese Kitchen Witch.

Chapter 2:

Holidays

Spring Time

Massa Sovada/Portuguese Sweet Bread

Like many cultures, themes of fertility and the new agrarian year are enmeshed within the socio-religious practices of the Portuguese people. One of the most common events to be looked forward to in the Spring is the making of Portuguese Sweet Bread, or Massa Sovada. Although Sweet Bread is a common dessert for the

Portuguese, the making of this bread is particularly meaningful in the Spring.

Sweet bread is one of the most commonly offered gifts to neighbors and friends, despite these same neighbors and friends having made plenty for themselves (and of course others!). As mentioned earlier, the gift is preceded with a verbal offering towards to the soul of a deceased, especially if a family member has passed earlier within the year or the year preceeding.

What makes spring time Sweet Bread so particularly special is the nest of eggs laid atop each loaf. Although the Portuguese do not color and hide eggs as is commonly done in the United States, the fertility symbol of eggs has also worked its way into the spring time ritual of the Portuguese. Follow the recipe below for a somewhat laborious yet all the worth while batch of homemade Portuguese Sweet Bread.

One thing to remember before making this recipe, or any of the others in this book is the temperament of the cook and the power that the Portuguese believe can be transferred from the cook to the product. Only make a recipe, especially one as labor intensive as Sweet Bread, when feeling positive or happy. Any negativity may spoil the rising of the dough, and any feelings of ill harm will undoubtedly be transferred through the bread to the recipient.

Massa Sovada

1/4 cup Water (warm for yeast)

1 cup Scalded milk

1 cup Sugar (add another ½ a cup for more sweetness if you like)

2 tsp of either (depending on your preference)

vanilla or lemon rind

1/2 cup Butter

1/2 tsp of salt

5 1/2 To 6 cups all-purpose flour

4 Eggs

2 packages yeast

6-8 previously hard boiled eggs (be careful to avoid any cracks while boiling).

Preheat oven to 350 degrees. Dissolve yeast in warm water. Scald milk and add to sugar, butter and salt; stir until butter is melted. Mix vanilla or lemon rind and flour.

Add 1/2 the flour to the milk/sugar/butter/salt, and mix until smooth. Beat 3 eggs and add them and the yeast to the mixture. Continue to add remaining flour to make soft dough. Remove from bowl and place on floured board. Knead until smooth and satiny (about 15 minutes). Shape into a ball and place in buttered bowl. Cover and let rise until double in size (2-1/2 to 3 hours).

Punch risen dough down and divide it in half, while putting aside a handful of dough to make the nest with. Place dough in two greased pans (8 inches round). The handful of dough can be placed on a plate for the time being. Let the two loaves and miscellaneous dough on the plate rise in a warm place until double in size (1-1/2 to 2 hours). Brush tops of dough in greased pans with remaining egg (beaten). Carefully place 3 hard boiled eggs on top of each sweet bread in the center. Using both hands, as you would with play dough, rub a small amount of the extra dough until a long spiral is formed, and place circularly around the eggs.

Bake in 350 degree oven for 20-30 minutes or until golden brown. Brush melted butter over cooked loaves for an attractive glossing. Let cool in pan, and carefully shake loose to release after completely cool. Slice generously and toast for a treat called Torrada. Otherwise, eat as a dessert the way it is. The twice cooked eggs are also delicious and are usually fought over.

Magical side note: *As you hard boil the eggs, be sure to ask the eggs for a wish or a wish for another person; something you want to come to be or a positive personality trait you wish gained (this is not the appropriate means for a banishment or removal spell). As the eggs harden, your magical request will come to be. Be sure the right person gets the correct egg, though!*

Biscoitos/Portuguese Biscotti

Unlike the Biscotti of many an espresso shop, Portuguese Biscoitos are circular and wreath shaped. The symbolism of the wreath represents life itself, and the circular cycles of the seasons within life. We all experience negativity and every year has a Winter. However, in the end the positive always returns, as does the Spring, and eating this sweet cookie is a reminder of that, as well as a means of carrying out the intention of many more "Springs."

Biscoitos

3 eggs

2 1/4 cups of sugar

1 cup of softened butter

1 cup of lukewarm milk

1 tsp of baking soda

3 1/2 tsp baking powder

½ tsp salt

7 cups of flour

1 1/2 tsp of vanilla or lemon rind

Preheat oven to 350. Combine all ingredients in a bowl. Using your hands as you would with play dough, roll palm fulls of dough into spirals approximately 7 inches long and approximately one finger in width. Connect the two ends to make a circular cookie, and place on a well greased cookie sheet. Bake for 18 minutes or until golden brown.

The Festa

Similar to the Spanish word most people are familiar with, a Portuguese Festa can be quite a party. Festas usually include plenty of food, drink, dance, and other forms of entertainment. Sometimes live animal auctions take place as well as games of gambling. A procession which wanders through the streets of costumed children and ornately embellished cows followed by a musical ensemble or brass band is the climax of the event which traditionally starts on a Friday night and ends on Sunday evening. The season of the Festa starts off in the Spring, usually on a weekend around the Vernal Equinox, or on what is commonly referred to by the Neo-Pagan community as Beltane, depending on the location. A Queen and her side maids become a central focus of the event. These are Portuguese girls who are members of the community and whose families are able to afford the lavish costumes and pageantry involved with being the Queen. The crowns are usually pure silver or gold plated, and can weigh in excess of several pounds.

Often times it is explained to newcomers that the Queen represents the Virgen Mary. However, once the main focus of the event is discovered, it quickly becomes clear that the tradition is based on Goddess worship for the sake of a prosperous agricultural season that year. In fact, the end of the Festa season usually closes with a bang, to include another weekend of dancing, food, drink, and merriment in celebration of the end of a prosperous agricultural year, taking place in the Fall.

Festas rotate locations through the agricultural season, with families traveling from community to community to take part in the celebration and ritual. In California, Festas take place in the many Portuguese communities from Eureka to the Los Angeles area and are designed to emulate as close as possible the traditions of the Festa back in the old country. If a community is wealthy enough, provided sufficient donations are made, all the festivities will be free of charge to anyone in attendance. At a minimum, the food, parade, and dance will be free to the public. These events take place at the local Portuguese Hall, which are large facilities on private property owned by the local Portuguese community.

One Portuguese Hall I have started visiting in the Central Valley of California, which includes three elaborate structures on several acres, was paid for in full by one Acorean immigrant and rancher whose daughter was born ill. This endeavor was taken on as a "promessa" or offering of sacrifice, that in return, his daughter become healthy.

The meat used for the steaks and Sopas (traditional soup served at a Festa) are either donated by the Portuguese farmers in the area, or purchased from Portuguese farmers via donations by the community. The sacrifice of making a donation is to ensure a prosperous harvest, and so families regardless of economic ability are certain to donate whatever they can. The animals are then blessed by a "priest" or other spiritual figure within the community, and then in the form of modern day animal sacrifice, the slaughtering of the animals for the celebratory meal is completed for all to share in.

The Portuguese Hall usually consists of a large main hall with kitchen facilities used for dining, a separate dance hall, and a chapel. During the weekend of the Festa, the chapel is decorated with flowers and brightly colored velvets, with the central focus being an enormous crown of pure silver, which always includes a matching silver wand or scepter. Candles lit with intentions and wishes are placed all around the crown with the hope that the Queen of Heaven will answer their prayers.

Centuries ago the Portuguese had to learn to conceal their pagan practices so as to appear Catholic to the Church, and avoid torture or death at the stake. Thus, themes of Mary as the Queen of Heaven became entwined with the existing practices, and often times the Festas were given titles having to do with Jesus. However, anyone attending any Festa even today will find there is little to no attention given to Jesus or even a male deity. The Queen and concept of a Holy Ghost remain the focus of the Festa.

Anyone interested in attending a Festa is always welcome, regardless of race or spiritual orientation. As I mentioned, these take place in Portugal, the Acores, and Madeira islands, as well as the Portuguese communities within some of the countries once held in possession by Portugal.

However, Portuguese immigrants in Canada and the U.S. have continued this tradition. At the time of this writing, there exists a website (www.festasonline.com) dedicated to maintaining a calendar of Festas in Canada and the U.S. Also, for those of you who know you live in or near a Portuguese community, be sure to look in the yellow pages for your local Portuguese Hall for dates in your area.

The Summer Solstice

The Summer Solstice, usually right in the middle of the Festa season, is another time for pageantry and fanfare. The Summer Solstice marks the midpoint of the agricultural season and in addition to a Festa with food, procession, and the like, it is also a time for divination and a deep connection to the spiritual world. It is believed that just as the plants and young livestock are coming to fulfillment, so to is the ability for one to predict what will happen to them in the year following.

Egg Divination

One example of the Portuguese belief in the divinatory powers of the Summer Solstice is the traditional practice of the egg divination. On the night of the Summer Solstice, fill a tall, clear glass with water approximately three-quarters of the way full. Preferably under the light of the moon, hold a raw egg above the glass and ask for the powers of the Summer Solstice to show you, through the egg, what will be for you in the year to come. Then, crack the egg allowing only the white of the egg into the glass of water. Let it sit overnight (again, preferably under the moonlight and usually on a window sill).

After a night's rest, check on your egg in the morning. Without moving the egg and water, gaze at the image the egg has formed for you. The first concept the picture or symbol brings to you will provide you with some insight into the year ahead. My mother and father both believe strongly in this and swear they both saw airplanes in their glass the year before they came to America. My mother also shares that she saw a church in her glass the summer before she married.

The Water of Summer Solstice

Referred to in Portugal as the Feast of Saint John, a Christian holiday taking place at the end of June and commonly referred to by many social scientists as the Christian attempt to blend new practices with the older Pagan traditions, water gathered on the Feast of Saint John is believed to hold great healing properties. In Portugal, children and cattle are forced into streams and other bodies of natural, running water to gain the purification and medicinal powers of the water on or around the Summer Solstice.

In the afternoon of the Summer Solstice, either bathe directly in naturally running water, or use recycled milk jugs to bring home some of this water. You may place it in the refrigerator to keep it fresh for up to several weeks, and add a drop of bleach to maintain freshness for longer than that.

Although it's preferential to bathe in the water on the Summer Solstice, the water is believed to hold its healing powers beyond the evening of the Summer Solstice so long as it is gathered that day.

Winter

As is the case with many modern cultures, the Christian holiday of Christmas has become a focus among communities, and a holiday interlaced with many Pagan practices and traditions, such as the Christmas tree and mistletoe. The Winter Solstice, the shortest day of the year, is a time of darkness, a time to reflect inward on our actions and events in the year behind us, and a time to look forward to the birth of the light once again.

"Boas Festas", meaning happy holidays, is the primary greeting among the Portuguese this time of year.

However, as was mentioned earlier, practices were often times moved from the Solstice to the Christmas holiday to prevent persecution, as proof the family practiced Catholicism and not Paganism. However, the Portuguese being rebellious by nature practice their Christmas on the 24th of December and not the 25th, which is usually closer to the Winter Solstice. Be sure to practice some of the easy rituals below for a traditional Portuguese Winter Solstice.

Presents in Your Shoes

As is the case with stockings, children in Portugal anxiously leave their shoes at the door or near the fireplace as a receptacle for presents from Father Winter. Although Santa Claus has managed to impose himself upon the culture, for those who accept the concept he is shown in blues, gold, and winter inspired attire rather than the red and green velvet Santa America has become familiar with.

Fogueira da Consoada

Similar to the concept of a Yule Log, the Fogueira da Consoada is burned on the night of the Winter Solstice to bring warmth and light to the family, both literally and magically speaking. It is best if a log is cut by a family member, and the log is often decorated by the family before burning. Be sure to get the log as hot as you can as a Fogueira da Consoada that goes out before the log is done burning is a sign of misfortune to come.

Once the Fogueira has burned completely, gather the ashes for safekeeping. Many Portuguese keep the ashes between their mattresses as a means of preventing ill harm upon the household until the following Winter Solstice, when it is returned to the earth when a new log is cut. Some Portuguese put the ashes away along with several pine cones from the season and burn them at a later time when the season becomes particularly stormy as a means of protecting the home from a lightening storm.

Crumbs for the Dead

This dark time of the year is a time to reflect upon and recall the dead. One practice, "Alminhas a Penar", involves leaving crumbs in front of the fireplace to invite the dead during the season in hopes that they bring the family fruits and grains in return during the following harvest season. After the Winter holiday has passed, be sure to carefully sweep-up any leftover crumbs and place them outside in the garden or forest, rather than throwing them away.

Another Winter tradition of the Portuguese involving the remembrance of the dead is based on the holiday meal eaten on the 24th of December. Whether your holiday meal is on Christmas Eve or the Winter Solstice, be sure to make a place setting at the table for the last deceased in your family. Provide servings of food and beverage as you would any guest, along with silverware and a chair.

Many Portuguese swear they have seen or experienced the presence of their dearly departed. Others believe this tradition to be a respectful way of assisting the deceased who have recently parted and who do not comprehend that they have left this world. The place setting gently demonstrates to the deceased that they are unable to partake of the meal, but that they remain in the loving memory of the family. This practice is similar to the tradition of the Dumb Supper held in many parts of the world, where a meal is eaten in silence and a deceased is summoned to attend.

Chapter 3:

Portuguese Herbal Remedies

The Portuguese are well known for their old wives tales and folk medicine, particularly in the country side and mountains where medical treatment may still be scarce. However, the results of some of their remedies is undeniable. Below are several examples with ingredients that should be fairly easy to come by either through your grocer, the local natural foods store, or the internet.

For Cough

Several leaves of "Salva" / Velvet leaf sage

Several tsp. Scotch or Whisky

4 Tbsp honey

1 Cup water

Boil the sage in the water until water begins to turn color. Take off the heat and add the remaining ingredients. Let sit for at least an hour.

Sweeten with more honey, if necessary, to accommodate your personal tastes.

Serve several tablespoons each hour for sore throat and cough.

For Rash

¼ Cup of lard

1 tsp ash, fireplace soot

½ tsp clove oil

¼ tsp dried mugwart

¼ tsp dried belladonna or mandrake leaves

½ tsp benzoin tincture

Using a mortar and pestle, crush the leaves until almost a powder.

In a small saucepan or cauldron, heat the lard on low until melted. Stir in the remaining ingredients and the benzoin as a preservative in clockwise motion for ten to fifteen minutes.

Place in a sealable container and let cool in the refrigerator, where it should be stored permanently.

Not for internal use.

***Magical side note:** This ointment for rash is also known as the magical flying belladonna of the dark ages and mystical tales. On the night of the full moon, try applying some of the ointment to your temples and "third eye", the area of the pineal gland located between both eyes. This is actually sold over the counter in pharmacies throughout Portugal still today.*

Remedy for Non-Migraine Headache

3 Red rose petals

Eucalyptus oil, Mentholatum will work

Rub eucalyptus oil on temples and location of your "third eye." Place the red rose petals over each area of oil, and lay down for a nap. This works best in a darkened room.

Other Commonly Used Remedies

The following list of commonly used remedies should be used at your discretion. If you have any medical issues, allergies, or are taking medication, discuss these frequently used folk treatments with your physician.

Anise – Make a potent tea from the seeds to remove excess mucus and other unhealthy substances from the gastrointestinal system.

Apple Juice – This common beverage is believed to serve as a liver detoxifier when ingested in large quantities over a period of a week. Drink 8 8oz. glasses of apple juice a day for a week when your body has been exposed to an overindulgence of unhealthy habits.

Egg White – Although not an herbal remedy, its' white is used to assist with facial acne and oily skin. Strain the white from the egg, rub on face, and let dry until your skin becomes taut feeling. Then gently wash off with a warm wash cloth.

Eucalyptus – Portugal is a major exporter of eucalyptus products. Eucalyptus is used to assist with respiratory ailments such as stuffy noses and congested chests. Rub pure eucalyptus oil, available at your local health food store, on your chest and below your nostrils to aid with breathing and sleep better during a cold or flu.

Garlic – Garlic is used to decrease blood pressure. To receive this benefit, eat several cloves of garlic daily, or if you cannot tolerate to eat garlic "straight", increase your fresh garlic intake significantly in the foods you eat. Garlic is also believed to be a natural antibiotic. Furthermore, crush raw cloves to use as a topical fungicide.

Hot Peppers – Encourage ingestion of peppers in food for those who suffer from circulatory disorders, or who tend to run cold. Fresh peppers are best, but powdered peppers sold in the spice section work, too.

Kelp or Seaweed – For the people of the Acores Islands, kelp and seaweed are essentially free food items. These vegetables of the sea contain nearly 30 minerals which are especially helpful to glandular function, such as the thyroid. When the glandular system works well, your metabolism works efficiently, and this means a higher rate of calories burned. Try it in soup!

Licorice – Licorice is used to help with childbirth and gynecological maladies. Licorice is also believed to decrease stress levels. Make a tea from the boiled roots.

Parsley – Commonly used to assist with bladder infections. Make a tea of fresh parsley and sip steadily over several days.

Peppermint – Peppermint is used to calm the stomach during periods of stomach upset or during the stomach flu. Sip slowly, so as to avoid further upsetting your stomach, in the form of a tea made from fresh leaves.

Port – This famous wine of Portugal is commonly ingested in small amounts after meals as it is believed to aid in the digestive process.

Sage – One of the most commonly used herbs among the Portuguese, sage assists with coughs, sore throats, and respiratory infections. As indicated in the recipe above, it is commonly steeped over a period of a day in a hard liquor to help break the beneficial components of this plant down.

Chapter 4:

Practical Magic

Home Blessing

Whether moving into a new home or for your current place of residence, a home blessing is essential to remove any negativity, unwanted spirits, or undesirable psychic activity which may have remained from prior to your arrival. There are several variations to home blessings most involving garlic and salt. Select the variation that most appeals to you and use it in your home.

*One method is to hang fresh garlic above all the windows and doors. It is believed the pungent odor will frighten away any negativity or evil, causing them to exit through the doors or windows and preventing any new agents from entering.

*Make a circle using sea salt, on the night of the full moon, around your house starting at the front door. The circle should be counter clockwise with the front door as 12. This direction will "undo" the negativity.

*Burn several large cloves of garlic in the oven over an hour or so, leaving the oven door slightly ajar so the smoke penetrates the entire home, purging the home of evil.

*For extreme circumstances, where an intense home cleaning is needed such as in cases of poltergeists or illness which will not depart despite medical care, be sure to place a few drops of ammonia in each of the four corners of each room of your home. Start in the back of the home, leaving the front door open, and work your way forward so as to slowly force the negativity forward and out the door. Although it may seem extreme, you can then wash your front porch with water containing urine. This will keep the negativity from ever crossing your threshold again.

Building a Shrine or Altar in the Home

Most Portuguese homes that have space will have a shrine of 3 tiers in the home. These are constructed of wood and look like a case of three stairs, with the top tier as the smallest (approximately 5 inches deep by 10 inches long) and increasing in size symmetrically downward. The tiers are then covered loosely in satin or another fine fabric, which can be changed to coordinate with the colors of the seasons, or to coordinate with the colors corresponding with the saint or spirit you are paying homage to. Often times, the base is covered in a white fabric is designated as the tier to pay homage to the ancestors, or "antepassados." The back is placed against

a wall. Cushions are usually placed on the floor in front of the shrine for comfort while sitting or kneeling.

The tops of each tier are usually quite cluttered with family photos, candles, items from nature, white Christmas lights as trim, flowers, and usually culminates with the top tier as the center of focus. If the family can afford the silver "coroa" (crown) mentioned in the section on Festas, this along with its matching silver scepter are placed at the top. A statue of your patron diety may also be placed atop the shrine.

An interesting side note, the island of Terceira in the Acores is reknowned for its Imperios, or "Holy Ghost Houses." Although the colorful Imperios of Terceira are most reknowned, all the communities of the Acores Islands have Imperios that either belong to the community, or to the owner of the property on which the Imperio sits. Personal devotion takes place in these mini-chapels, where the shrine inside is constructed as was described above. Many of these chapels have some form of the image of a crown at the top, and all are brightly painted. Family ceremony and rituals take place in these Imperios. Some believe the community church was attended by individuals who had to publicly demonstrate their Catholicism in order to save their lives. But, in the privacy of their Imperios, they could practice their magical traditions as they pleased.

Protection Against the Evil Eye

The evil eye is believed to be able to attack anything; objects, people, and animals. Babies and small children are particularly at risk of the evil eye. Often times, villagers know exactly who has the evil eye and know to avoid them, or make appropriate protections when encountering them. However, this is not always known, and particularly in a country as large as America can be impossible. Thus, wearing a charm purchased or made of clay in the shape of a fig, symbolic of a woman's genitalia, may provide protection.

A well regarded secret in the protection of the evil eye is the rue tree "arruda." If you cut a leaf or sprig from a rue, be sure to leave something in its place. This offering, a "penhora", can be a cloth, button, or other small object. This offering prevents the rue from drying up and dieing. If you find a rue with an unusual object laying next to it, you now know why! Another use for ruc is to carry several leaves behind the ear. In doing so, the wearer ensures that envy is kept at bay.

To protect her newborn from the evil eye, a Portuguese mother will lick her baby's head three times reciting the following:

"I gave birth to you, I raised you, the fright and

the evil eye I remove from you.

The cow licks her calf because of love,

And I lick [remove] your fright and evil eye."

Or in its old-Portuguese form:

"Te pari, te crie, o espanto e

o olho mau eu tira de ti.

O vaca lambe su bezerrinho por amor,

E eu te lambo oesptanto e olho mau."

The protective hand gesture against the evil eye has several forms. The most common form is actually practiced among other Mediterranean cultures and involves making a fist with one hand, while covering the thumb with the forefinger so the thumb pushes up between the forefinger and the middle finger (see page 16). This is also called the fig or "figa" and again is symbolic of the female genitalia. Secretly make this fist if you believe to be in the presence of the evil eye.

The other hand gesture has its roots in the Sephardic traditions among the Moors and Jews who once widely inhabited all of Portugal. If you believe you are in the presence of such negativity or someone with the evil eye outright curses you, quickly raise your right hand upward with all five fingers stretched apart, palm up and yell "Os cinco! Os Cinco!" (The five! The five!) twice. The five represents the five fingers of your hand and the five fingers of the Hamsa which is a magical symbol and amulet of protection. Oddly enough, my father uses "os cinco" as a jestful defense when I tease him. He and probably many other contemporary Portuguese believe this to be a lighthearted threat to strike someone when they call you a name or poke fun at you. How tradition carries on in cryptic practices!

To Remove a Curse

Since infants are incapable of removing curses placed upon them, as was instructed above, lick the forehead of the infant three times, and this time quickly spit onto the ground your saliva after licking. It is believed among the Portuguese that infants, pregnant women, and breastfeeding mothers are among the most vulnerable as many sterile individuals or individuals who wish they were married (especially to your spouse) may wish illness to the baby, the baby to become riddled with colic, or the mother to dry of her breast milk.

As an adult, there are numerous ways to remove a curse. The best method for self removal is to take a bath every night between the full moon and the new moon. The bath should be made with cool to cold water so as to still the curse, not invigorate it. In the bath should be leaves of rue, rosemary, and cloves of garlic. Be sure to scrub every bit of yourself with this water starting with your head and working your way down. Do not exit the bath without standing up, turning clocking wise three times, releasing the plug, and watching the contaminated water leave your body and tub, down into the drain. Let your body air dry and do not remove any herbs which may stick to your body. The remaining herbs which will not make it down the drain should be buried the next day.

To Attract a Mate

If your desire is to begin a romance with someone you know, or to obtain a new level of romance with your current partner, the following should work. Using the sweet bread recipe found later in this book, place a toasted piece in the shape of a crow into your desired's coffee. However, be sure the person you are placing the spell on does not find out, or instead of romance a strong aversion toward you will develop.

If you have a mate that you wish to enter into marriage with, yet he or she has failed to ask the question up to this point, the following is guaranteed to work. Decide what your least favorite color is. Then, on the night of a full moon, make a promise that if your lover asks for your hand in marriage, you will wear your least favorite color for your entire first year of marriage. You must be serious about doing this. If you are not serious or will not adhere to your promise, this will not work. If you are serious, and marry your beloved, be sure to stick to your promise. To break it early will result in a long but tumultuous marriage.

Another method to obtain a marriage proposal is to cut a lock of your hair and secretly sew it into the seam of your beloved's pants. Be certain these are pants he or she will wear often.

If you are single and seek a romance, then this next simple spell will work. However, be certain this is what you want and be particular about the characteristics you want in a mate. Sometimes, we get what we ask for, and it's not always what we want in the end. On the evening of a full moon, go to a moving stream or river and prick the tip of your wedding ring finger so that three drops of blood fall into the moving water. The water will carry your intention to the seas and the result will be the mate of your dreams.

Images representing a traditional depiction of the
Mother of the Sea, referred to as Iemanja or
Yemanja in Brasil.

Of Seas and Cures

On the topic of the seas, it is most important to learn several things about the ocean. The ocean, the life source of the planet, is mother healer when it comes to muscular and bone ailments. Salt water is some of the best medicine for arthritis and other similar ailments. Be sure to bring some home in jugs, but not without leaving a token of appreciation to the mother sea for her gift of medicine. Whenever taking anything from the sea, be sure to first throw in seven pennies as a gift for her abundant goodness.

Also, did you ever learn that there is a correct way to enter the ocean? Indeed! To enter the ocean face forward is an affront to this maternal goddess, and a sign of aggression. It is wise to not challenge the forces of the sea, as she will always be the winner. Instead, enter the sea at a ninety degree angle, with your right side toward the water and your left toward the sand. Side step or hop sideways in until you are about waist deep, and then you can feel free to turn any direction you'd like.

Chapter 5:

More Traditional Recipes

Be sure to enjoy these traditional Portuguese recipes as an offering to a friend or neighbor for the souls of your departed, or just as a family treat. As mentioned in the section on Sweet Bread, always be sure to make the recipe in a pleasant mood and with plenty of time so as not to feel rushed. Feelings of tension or anger while cooking have been known to void the rising properties of yeast, to sour dough, and make tart the sweetest of desserts.

In Portuguese tradition, make your food with love and while feeling positive so as to promote these sentiments through the ingestion of the food you've served. Serving food to another that has been prepared while feeling angered or frustrated may result in the transmission of negativity to the person eating.

Arroz Doce / Portuguese Rice Pudding

2 cups water

1 cup short-grain rice (try your hardest to avoid long grain rice)

¼ teaspoon of table salt

2 cups of milk, scalded

zest of 1 lemon, without pith

1 cup sigar

Ground cinnamon for decorating

Pour the water into a 2 1/2 quart pan, cover and bring to a boil over medium-high heat. Stir in the rice with the salt and reduce heat to medium-low. Cover and simmer the rice for 20 to 25 minutes or until the water is nearly evaporated. Rice will be barely tender.

Stir in the warm milk and add the lemon peel. Stirring, continue to simmer until the mixture starts to thicken slightly, about 20 minutes. When the rice is well cooked, stir in the sugar and continue cooking until the sugar is dissolved and the pudding has thickened to the consistency of oatmeal, about 5 minutes more. Remove the pot from the heat. It will continue to thicken as it cools.

Pour or ladle the pudding onto a large serving platter or individual flat plates to a thickness of about 3/4 of an inch. (It will cool faster on flat dishes). Taking a pinch of ground cinnamon between thumb and forefinger, rub thumb and finger together gently and close to the surface of the rice. Slowly letting the cinnamon fall, dust the surface of the rice in a design of your choice, perhaps forming the initials of a guest or a holiday greeting. (If fingers are held too high, the cinnamon will scatter over a wider area). Cool and serve or chill the rice to serve later.

Magical side note: *Use the cinnamon as a means to inscribe a word or phrase that you wish to have come to fruition. If this is something you wish to have happen which involves a guest you will be serving the sweet rice to, and do not wish to have them see your word or phrase, use the sigil concept of spell working. With sigils, spells are turned into symbols which the subconscious knows, but is not familiar to the eye. You may do this by removing all the vowels out of a word which symbolizes the spell phrase to you. Turn the remaining consonants into a symbol you find appealing. Use the cinnamon to decorate this symbol on top of the sweet rice. Feed the rice to those you want to have this come to fruition on.*

Malasadas / Portuguese Donuts

½ cup milk

1 yeast cake or packet

1 ¼ cups sugar

2 tablespoons lukewarm water

½ teaspoon salt

¼ cup butter, melted

3 eggs

2 ¾ cups flour

Sugar to roll fried donut in

1 quart oil for frying

Heat milk to lukewarm. Moisten yeast in lukewarm water. Add the yeast, salt, sugar and melted butter to the milk. Stir in part of the flour, beating well with a wooden spoon to prevent lumps. Add beaten eggs and remaining flour to form a soft dough. Cover the dough and sit in warm place until doubled.

Heat oil to 350 degrees. Drop dough by tablespoonful into the hot oil and fry until evenly browned. Drain on absorbent paper and roll in sugar.

Magical side note: *While frying the Malasadas, keep an eye out for large bubbles which may form. Do not poke the air out of the bubbles. These are a sign of good luck for whoever eats that Malasada and to poke the bubble while cooking would release the luck.*

Alcatra / Portuguese Roasted Meat Dish

1 Beef rump roast or other roast

1 Stick of Linguica Sausage sliced into ¼" circles

4 Chicken breasts

½ Cup red wine, or 7-UP if you refrain from alcohol

¼ Cup sugar

1 small can of tomato sauce

2-3 Bay leaves

1 Clove of garlic

2 tsp Paprika

2 Onions, peeled and chopped large

3-4 Pepper corns

Salt to taste

Enough water to cover the roast

The dish is traditionally stewed in an oven in a clay pot. However, I find that the American alternative of the crock pot works splendidly.

Place all the ingredients in the pot, cover, and let simmer for 4-5 hours on medium-high over three days, placing pot in the refrigerator after each cooking session at the end of the day. Stir to ensure even coverage of sauce over meat. This will undoubtedly be the most tender meat you have ever tasted.

Alcatra is traditionally served over white, short-grain rice.

Magical side note: *Take note of how this dish is stewed over three days. Not only does this ensure an incredibly tender dish, but the number three holds mystical significance in the Portuguese culture. Prepare this dish three days before your next magical gathering or holiday feast and watch the magic spew forth from the cauldron to the guests!*

Caldo Verde / Green Soup

6 Potatoes, chopped for soup

1 Clove of garlic

2 Quarts of water

4 Tbsp olive oil

1 Stick of linguica, chopped paper thin (omit if you are vegetarian)

1 lb of collards, kale, or turnip greens

salt to taste

     Boil potatoes and water for a light broth, keeping as light as possible. Add linguica, garlic, and salt and let simmer.

Roll the greens and chop thinly into a skillet, scalding the greens to turn them bright green. Add the scalded greens and olive oil to the broth and let boil for five minutes.

For softer greens, you may allow soup to sit until desired softness.

Magical side note: *The color green denotes images of money, growth, harvest, and fertility to many cultures. As a means to bringing money to your family, particularly during a period of financial draught, make this inexpensive soup with a well cleansed dollar bill inserted into the broth for a portion of its cooking. You will be amazed at how well the dollar bill will fare.*

Chapter 6:

Portuguese Superstitions / Folklore

When walking across a room with children lying on the floor, be extremely cautious to avoid stepping over a child. This will stunt the child's growth. If you accidentally start to step over the child, but remember midway to stop, carefully retrace your steps back over the child.

When entering a home or business, be sure to always enter and exit through the same door.

Do not kill or strike crickets, particularly in the home. These creatures are a sign of good luck and to harm them would result in misfortune to you and yours.

If you are contemplating marriage, or the fruits of your love spell come to be, make certain to schedule your wedding on a Saturday. Fridays are bad luck for weddings, and Sundays are only so-so. If at all possible, schedule the event on a Saturday. A Saturday with a full moon is terrific. A Saturday that falls on a Solstice or Equinox is even better.

The rooster is an omen of good luck. If one mysteriously appears where one shouldn't, do not shoo it away. Make every attempt to avoid hitting a rooster with your car when driving. Keep a statue or icon of a rooster in your kitchen to attract luck.

Do not place your purse on the floor. Your financial situation will worsen. Always store your purse above ground level.

Do not eat with money on the table. This is a sign of gluttony and a challenge to the forces that bring you good fortune. Remove coins, paper money, and wallets from table before starting your meal.

With new life comes many blessings. Whether you are pregnant, or a friend or coworker is expecting, be sure to plan on purchasing an item of jewelry to adorn the newborn immediately after birth as this will bring you good fortune and a return on your investment on the spiritual and financial realms. A standard and unisex item given to newborns is a gold or silver bracelet that their name can be engraved on.

When grieving the loss of a recently departed loved one, be sure to refrain from calling their name out loud for the first year and a day after their death. It is quite common for the newly deceased to not quite realize they are no longer among the living and want to return home to continue living with those they love; hence the many stories of ghostly visits and apparitions we hear of. By openly grieving, we show them our loss, letting them know they are departed. By calling their name and speaking to them too soon after their departure from this realm may confuse them into believing they are still with us.

After a year and a day, our blood relatives should have arrived in the spirit realm successfully understanding that they are in the next phase of the cycle we call life. At this point, feel free to build a small altar covered in white cloth with a white candle and pictures of your blood relatives. It is commonly believed that a glass bowl of water (never metal) serves as a conduit to carry our messages to them. Make this altar as beautiful as you like, with items that remind you of them next to their photos. Be sure to spend time and talk to them about your life, your hopes, and your concerns. They are watching you and it is believed that if you open the door by inviting them into your life, they will provide you with much protection and benefit.

Keep a horseshoe hanging above your doors for good luck. Some believe the horseshoe can be hung however you'd like, while others hold strong to the belief that the horseshoe must be open end up, to keep the luck inside.

Keep a cauldeira, a small three legged cauldron, behind your front door for protection. Traditions vary with this practice, but you may fill it with garlic; burn incense in it; fill it with old nails, horseshoes, and other metal objects you find on your property; or place fresh rosemary in it.

When you've lost an item and just can't seem to locate it, be sure to invoke the helpful locating powers of Maria Queimada (Kay-mah-tha). Her name literally means Maria who is burned. Maria Queimada is actually Vita Kimpa, also referred to as Dona Beatriz, from the Congo. Dona Beatriz was initiated in the Congo spirituality, endowing her with great gifts of mediumship with the spirits. She eventually became a spiritual leader among her people and is sometimes called the Joan of Arc of Africa. She and her infant son were burned at the stake for heresy, in what is termed an auto de fe. The people of the Acores with their close connections to Angola and the Congo, invoke her to locate lost documents, keys, and other important items. Be sure to thank her once she's taken you to your missing item.

An aged, but still recognizable

sketch of Mama Kimpa Vita, also known as

Dona Beatriz.

Color Magic

Portuguese color magic can be used with almost anything. Use the following color correlations when working with colors or herbs, or buying flowers to place in front of your favorite religious statue.

Certain colors have strong connections to the energies of nature and you can invoke those energies to work for you, such as asking the ocean to wash away your stress. Colors also have connections to things we might request, as was indicated with the Caldo Verde recipe, with green having a connection to money

I'd like to note that in the US our currency happens to be green, so the connection is easy to make. However, in other nations where the currency is not green, or in ancient times when the currency was not even on paper, the connection to fortune still held in that green is the color of the trees and trees provide for us with fruit. Thus, these connections are ancient and strong; be sure you really want what you ask for.
White – Use white when working with blessings, cleansings, protection, and purification requests. White is also the fabric and candle color used for the alter when working with the spirits or the ancestors in Espiritismo.

Black – For work against enemies, cursing, and to break-up relationships. Obviously, this is quite ominous sounding and to be used at your own risk. There are times when black is positive, but since this book is a primer, we will only cover the basics in Portuguese magic.

Purple – To be used in efforts toward spiritual and psychic development, dreams, and to control the will of another for a temporary purpose.

Blue – For calming and to settle down uprising and heated feelings. Blue can be used to wash away illness in conjunction with the purification of white.

Red – Red, as is typically thought, is to be used for love, passion, and relationships. Red is invigorating with regard to issues of the heart.

Green – As mentioned earlier, green is associated with money, bountiful rewards, and returns. Green can be used any time you seek an increase whether it be in pay, gambling investment, or in conjunction with red to increase your family size.

Some wishes require a change in behavior that can't be expected to happen overnight. So, incorporate long term practices into your color magic that will strengthen your spell AND make you more aware of your intention. Several examples would be praying each day at the exact same time over a novena candle which usually burns for seven days, touching a ribbon of the particular color hanging from your front door every time you enter and exit your home, or hanging something such as a rabbit's foot dyed in the corresponding color from your car's mirror as a reminder to be mindful of your request every time you drive.

Incorporating this long term mindfulness is essential when battling lifelong burdens, obstacles imposed on you by others, or when you face opposition to meeting your desired outcome.

Dictionary of Portuguese Magical Terms & Concepts

Alma – Soul. Alminha is an endeared way of saying soul. The "inha" ending added to a word signifies attachment or endearment, as in the way one would make a word more appealing to a child.

Axe' – (The "x" makes an "sh" sound in Portuguese). The Portuguese spelling of an African word which literally means the energy of the Gods. However, the word has become so entwined in everyday usage that it can be used to mean "sense, feel, anticipate, or hope" as in "Eu axe bem" or "Eu axe sim" meaning "I think it's a good idea" or "I hope so."

Cauldeira – Cauldron.

Cantigas – Singing, songs, or chants.

Cigana - Gypsy. Like witch, replace the ending "a" with an "o" for the masculine.

Encantada – Magic or spell; to be under a trance. Most commonly used in casual conversation when someone is so ecstatic with an event, they are enchanted.

Espiritismo-A practice and belief system, usually passed down through generations, which believes in communication with the deceased living in the spirit realm. The philosophy also includes the belief in reincarnation, the possibility of mediumship for most individuals, reverence for the ancestors who have passed, and the goal of spirit perfection for all living and deceased spirits. This philosophy is practiced all over the world in various forms, but was formally made a doctrine by Allan Kardec. Thus, it is sometimes referred to as Kardecism . The English word for Espiritismo is Spiritism, which does take on a slightly different tone in American culture.

Equinocio – Equinox.

Erva – Herb.

Espirito – Spirit or ghost.

Estrela – Star.

Fadas – Fairies.

Fado – Fate. Fate is such an integral component of the belief system of the Portuguese that the world renowned style of soulful music sung in Portuguese and made famous by Amalia Rodrigues is called Fado.

Feiticeira, Jeitiera, Bruxa – The female form of several words meaning "Witch" or more correctly, "Sorceror." To make masculine, replace the ending "a" with an "o."

Feiticeiria, Jeitieria, Bruxeria – Witchcraft, sorcery.

Filha de Santo/Filho de Santo – Literally, Daughter or Son of the Saint. Most Portuguese children probably recall hearing their parents or grandparents let out this statement with a sigh of frustration. This term originates from the African syncretic religious practices, such as are commonly associated with the religions of Umbanda or Candomble. Individuals are believed to be born as a child of a Saint, or actually, Orixa who were syncretized as Catholic Saints during times of persecution. When a child is called this now, it is out of frustration, but also with a tinge of endearment because the child is displaying the personal qualities of the Saint, which can at times be contrary to what the parent desires of the child in compliance to house rules.

Invejar – To envy, desire strongly, or grudgingly admire. In this culture envy is seen as such a strong feeling, it is feared and believed to be the basis of many illnesses, break-ups, and other unexplained phenomenon. It is believed that envy can get the best of us, and so whether it is the person's intention or not, these negative effects can occur, so it is best to keep intentions secret or one's metaphorical chickens hidden until they hatch.

Lobishomens – Werewolves. The Portuguese who live in the forested hills of the northern mainland hold to their belief in werewolves. Do not confuse the ending "omens" with the English word meaning prophecy. Rather, the ending of the Portuguese Lobishomens is homens, the latin derived word for man, as in "homo sapien."

Mae de Santo – Mother of the Saint, literally. See Filha/o de Santo above. In the African syncretic practices of Umbanda and Candomble, which hold a matriarchal approach in its hierarchy, a Mae de Santo is the leader of the spiritual house; a priestess. As is the case with Filha/o de Santo, a woman may be called Mae de Santo half out of frustration when angering others or becoming bossy and demanding. You may hear a husband respond, "O, Mae de Santo!" to his wife's demands. Yes, there are also Pai de Santos.

Magico – Magic or magician.

Mar – Ocean, sea, salt water body.

Malvado – Evil, wicked.

Mau Olhado – Evil Eye.

Meia noite – Midnight.

Milagro – Miracle.

Misterio – Mystery.

Mortos – The dead, deceased.

Ovo – Egg.

Penar – Suffer(ing).

Promessa - Literally translated, a promise. However, a promessa is often an offering or sacrifice for a desire or spell work.

Sacrificio – Sacrifice.

Sangue – Blood.

Solsticio – Solstice.

Sonho(s) – Dream(s).

Susto – A scare or a fright, but spoken of as something one catches like a virus, such as "I caught a fright" or "Eu apenhei um susto." Several cultures believe in this concept of catching fright and the American Psychological Association has now, in an effort to better facilitate cultural understanding in treatment, incorporated the concept of "susto" and its symptoms into client experiences and treatment methodologies.

Vela – Candle.